RANDY'S
CORNER

DAY BY DAY WITH...

SERENA WILLIAMS

BY
TAMMY GAGNE

Mitchell Lane
PUBLISHERS

P.O. Box 196
Hockessin, Delaware 19707
Visit us on the web: www.mitchelllane.com

Copyright © 2016 by Mitchell Lane Publishers, Inc. All rights reserved. No part of this book may be reproduced without written permission from the publisher. Printed and bound in the United States of America.

Printing   1   2   3   4   5   6   7   8   9

RANDY'S CORNER
DAY BY DAY WITH. . .

Adam Jones	Justin Bieber
Alex Morgan	LeBron James
Beyonce	Manny Machado
Bindi Sue Irwin	Mia Hamm
Calvin Johnson	Miley Cyrus
Carrie Underwood	Missy Franklin
Chloë Moretz	Selena Gomez
Dwayne "The Rock" Johnson	Serena Williams
Elena Delle Donne	Shakira
Eli Manning	Shaun White
Gabby Douglas	Stephen Hillenburg
Jennifer Lopez	Taylor Swift
	Willow Smith

Library of Congress Cataloging-in-Publication Data
Gagne, Tammy.
 Day by day with Serena Williams / by Tammy Gagne.
     pages cm. — (Randy's corner)
 Includes bibliographical references and index.
 ISBN 978-1-68020-111-6 (library bound)
 1. Williams, Serena, 1981– —Juvenile literature. 2. Tennis players—United States—Biography—Juvenile literature. 3. African American women tennis players—Biography—Juvenile literature. I. Title.
 GV994.A2G34 2015
 796.342092—dc23
 [B]
                                                                 2015012938
eBook ISBN: 978-1-68020-112-3

ABOUT THE AUTHOR: Tammy Gagne has written dozens of books for children, including *Missy Franklin* and *Hope Solo* for Mitchell Lane Publishers. She resides in northern New England with her husband and son. One of her favorite pastimes is visiting schools to speak to kids about the writing process.

DAY BY DAY WITH

SERENA WILLIAMS

Serena Williams was just twelve when her father Richard predicted that she and her sister Venus would become the world's top two tennis players. Some people saw him as a proud father. Others thought he pushed the girls. But he was right.

SERENA POSES FOR THE CAMERAS HOLDING HER THIRD US OPEN TROPHY.

Serena Jameka Williams was born in Saginaw, Michigan on September 26, 1981. Even then, Richard had a plan for her. Knowing how much money the best tennis players made, he taught his daughters to play at just four years old.

SERENA WILLIAMS

Being older, Venus had a head start. But Serena wasted no time catching up. Both girls turned professional at fourteen. Serena won the US Open in 1999—and Wimbledon

VENUS
WILLIAMS

in 2000. Venus too was successful. They
became the only sisters in history to have
won Grand Slam titles.

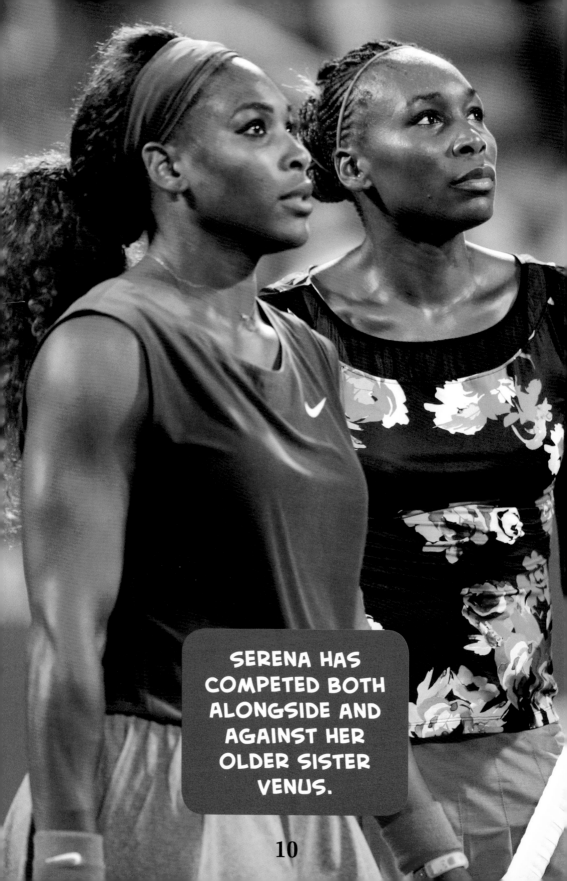

SERENA HAS COMPETED BOTH ALONGSIDE AND AGAINST HER OLDER SISTER VENUS.

The media enjoys comparing Serena and Venus. Who is the better player? In titles, Serena wins the competition hands down. Serena has also won more prize money, totaling about sixty million dollars. Venus once ruled the game. But Serena keeps ruling it.

THE SISTERS SHARED A TROPHY AT THE 2009 US OPEN.

Both sisters love tennis, and it helped them prove themselves. But today tennis is just one aspect of their many talents. From endorsement deals to their own companies, the Williams sisters are a force to be reckoned with on and off the court.

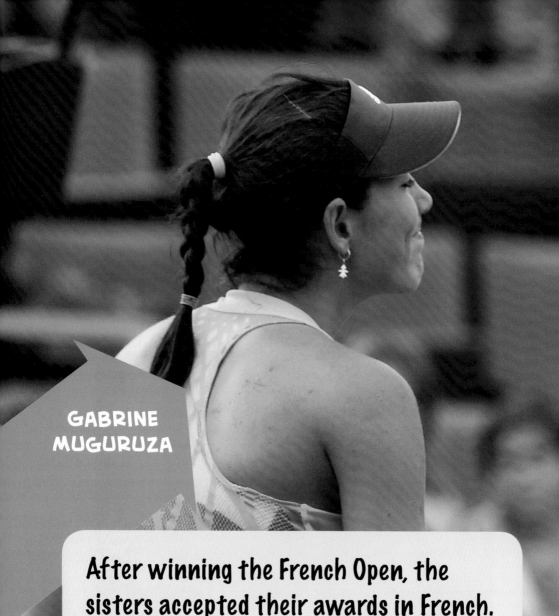

After winning the French Open, the sisters accepted their awards in French. They had seen another player do the same thing. "Venus and I decided that when we got there, we'd also be able to speak French," Serena told Oprah Winfrey in 2003.

SERENA SHAKES HANDS WITH GABRINE FOLLOWING THEIR MATCH.

As clothing designers, Serena and Venus are known for their bold outfits. Venus explained to Oprah. "Serena and I went to fashion

design school, so we're not just walking around saying, 'We want to be fashion girls.' We're actually educated in the matter."

SERENA AND
VENUS DESIGN
THEIR OWN
CLOTHES.

SERENA GETS
PICKED UP
AFTER
WINNING YET
ANOTHER
TOURNAMENT

When Serena won her Olympic gold medal in doubles, she was able to share the victory with her sister. "We're looking forward to Rio," Serena told the *Huffington Post* shortly after the win, "and trying to get some sort of medal there."

In 2013, at the age of thirty-one, Serena became the oldest female player to be ranked number one in tennis. Following the accomplishment, Serena Tweeted, "Thanks everyone for all the support. Back to number one. #1 and it feels so good. Serena #1."

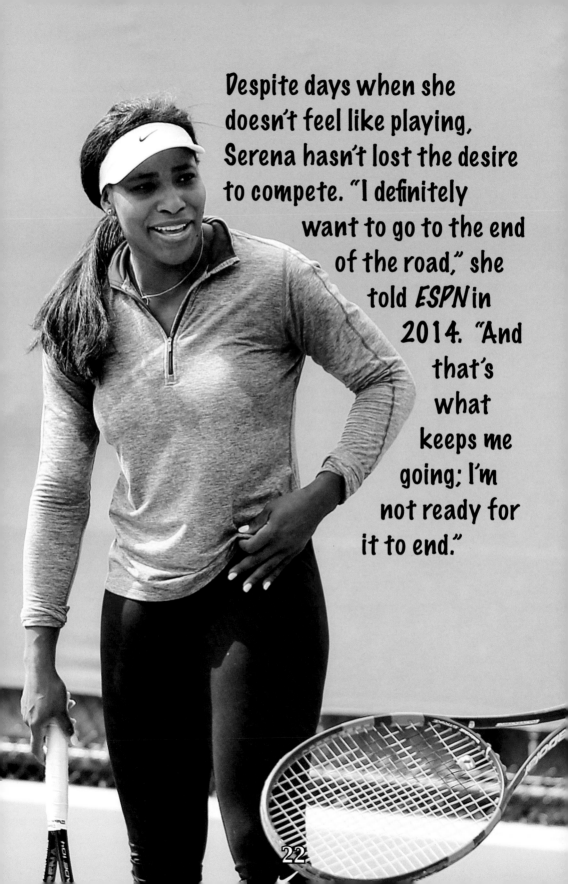

Despite days when she doesn't feel like playing, Serena hasn't lost the desire to compete. "I definitely want to go to the end of the road," she told *ESPN* in 2014. "And that's what keeps me going; I'm not ready for it to end."

SERENA'S
COACH PATRICK
MOURATOGLOU

SERENA CELEBRATES ANOTHER WIN

24

Continuing to compete in her thirties won't be easy. But even when she suffers a defeat, Serena knows she has the best support system available. "I have a sister, and she knows exactly what I'm going through," Serena told *Sports Illustrated* in 2014.

SERENA WILLIAMS AND
HER FATHER RICHARD WILLIAMS

The sisters have celebrated many victories together. But in 2003, the sisters suffered a personal loss. Their half-sister, Yetunde Price was murdered. Serena has said how unfair the whole ordeal was. "[O]ur family has always been positive and we always try to help people," she told the *Los Angeles Times*.

SERENA AND VENUS POSE OUTSIDE THE VANITY FAIR OSCAR PARTY IN 2012.

SERENA RAN IN THE SERENA WILLIAMS FOUNDATION QUARTER-MARATHON HERSELF.

Serena dealt with her grief by helping others. In 2008 she established the Serena Williams Foundation. The charity helps American children who have been affected by violent crimes. In 2014 the organization hosted a quarter-marathon to raise money for the charity.

SERENA IS A FASHION ICON BOTH ON AND OFF THE TENNIS COURT.

Everyone is wondering whether Serena will be able to come out on top again. The legendary Billie Jean King told *Sports Illustrated,* "I think Serena is probably our best athlete ever . . . but she's still got to earn the titles. She's got to win and she knows it."

FURTHER READING

FIND OUT MORE

Beard, Hilary, Serena Williams, and Venus Williams. *Venus and Serena: Serving From The Hip: 10 Rules for Living, Loving, and Winning.* Boston: HMH Books for Young Readers, 2005.

Donaldson, Madeline. *Venus & Serena Williams.* Minneapolis: Lerner Publications, 2011.

Serena Williams Foundation http://www.theserenawilliamsfoundation.org/

_____. *Sports Illustrated Kids Big Book of Who: ALL-STARS: The 101 Stars Every Fan Needs to Know.* New York: Sports Illustrated Kids, 2014.

WORKS CONSULTED

Conway, Tyler. "Serena Williams Will Become the Oldest Top-Ranked Woman Ever After Qatar Open." *Bleacher Report.* February 15, 2013. http://bleacherreport.com/articles/1530896-serena-williams-will-become-oldest-top-ranked-woman-ever-after-qatar-open

Corbett, Melissa Lawrence. "Serena Williams Further Distinguishes Herself from Big Sister Venus Williams." *Bleacher Report.* June 12, 2013. http://bleacherreport.com/articles/1594536-serena-williams-further-distinguishes-herself-from-big-sister-venus-williams

Evert, Chris. "Impact 25: Serena Williams Serves Up Some Ambitious Goals for 2015." *ESPN The Magazine.* December 17, 2014. http://espn.go.com/espnw/news-commentary/article/12005414/serena-williams-serves-some-ambitious-goals-2015

McCauley, Janie. "Serena, Venus Williams Win Historic Third Women's Doubles Olympic Tennis Gold Medal." *Huffington Post.* October 5, 2012. http://www.huffingtonpost.com/2012/08/05/serena-venus-williams-olympics-tennis-doubles_n_1743600.html

Porter, Kevin. "Serena Williams completes Ultimate Run for charity." *Examiner.com.* December 16, 2014. http://www.examiner.com/article/serena-williams-completes-ultimate-run-for-charity

Price, S.L. "Was Serena's odd Wimbledon a sign of final fade or fuel for resurgence?" *Sports Illustrated.* August 25, 2014. http://www.si.com/tennis/2014/08/25/serena-williams-us-open

"Serena Williams Fast Facts." CNN. September 8, 2014. http://www.cnn.com/2013/09/13/us/serena-williams-fast-facts/

Suarez, Kelly-Anne. "Tennis Star Serena Williams Addresses Half Sister's Killer." *Los Angeles Times.* April 7, 2006. http://articles.latimes.com/2006/apr/07/local/me-sentence7

Winfrey, Oprah. "Oprah Talks to Venus and Serena Williams." *O Magazine.* March 2003. http://www.oprah.com/omagazine/Oprahs-Interview-with-Venus-and-Serena-Williams

INDEX